PARENTING KIDS WITH AUTISM:
A modern guide on how to handle kids with autism.

Eric E. Honaker

Table of content

Chapter 1

Meaning and the true nature of autism.

Autism, sometimes known as classic autism or autistic disorder, is a developmental illness that affects a person's physical, social, and verbal abilities. It usually manifests before the age of three. Eugen Bleuler, a Swiss psychiatrist, first used the word autism (derived from the Greek autos, which means "self") to characterize retreat into one's inner world, a behavior he saw in people with schizophrenia, in 1911. In 1943, American psychiatrist Leo Kanner, who was born in Austria, separated the illness from schizophrenia and coined the term "autism" to characterize it.

Autism spectrum disorder is a disorder.

Identification and frequency

Asperger syndrome, classic autism, and pervasive developmental disorder not otherwise defined (PDD-NOS) are all grouped under the term "autism spectrum disorders," which refers to a group of illnesses (ASDs). Individuals with Asperger syndrome often do not have significant cognitive impairments, in contrast to those with classic autism, and their IQ is in the normal or even high range. They also don't show any signs of a language learning deficit. Some, but not all, of the typical autistic symptoms, are present in people with PDD-NOS.

The incidence of autism varies greatly across and within nations, despite the best estimates being available. This is partly because of variations in available resources and diagnostic criteria. For instance, it was discovered that 1 in every 185 people in one area of the United Kingdom had an ASD. However, in the same part of the nation, it was discovered that the frequency of classic autism varied between 1 in 250 and 1 in 400 people. The incidence of autism seems to have dramatically increased globally between the mid-1900s and the early 2000s as well. Although the adoption of wider diagnostic criteria or other variables may have contributed to the rise, it is unknown if there has been an increase in the incidence of the condition. The National Health

Interview Survey (NHIS), for instance, is one of several various monitoring techniques used to ascertain the incidence of ASD in the United States. Parent-reported diagnosis of ASDs in children increased as a result of modifications to the NHIS's ASD questions in 2014, including their rewording and extension for more information.

Potential causes and dangers

The etiology of autism remains uncertain. However, it seems that the condition is influenced by both hereditary and environmental factors. According to a 2011 research that examined twin pairs in whom at least one twin had an ASD, environmental variables were more important in determining vulnerability than genetic ones, which only contribute little. According to another study, men and females have different genetic susceptibilities to autism, with females needing more mutations than males to develop the disorder. The so-called female protective paradigm, which aims to explain why autism is more common in men, is supported by women's stronger genetic resistance to it. The environment and gene interactions most likely have a significant impact on an individual's predisposition to autism.

Maternal infection during pregnancy has been suggested as an environmental risk factor for autism and other ASDs. Indeed, some maternal infections have been linked to a higher prevalence of neurodevelopmental problems in kids, such as schizophrenia and autism. The mother's immune system becomes active when she contracts diseases like the rubella virus, and this immunological activity during the first trimester of pregnancy has been linked to harm to the developing brain of the embryo or baby.

Studies involving siblings have provided important insights into the heritability of autism. For instance, researchers discovered a region on chromosome 15 that is deleted or duplicated in certain autistic individuals. Defects in and close to this area have also been linked to other diseases of neuronal development, such as Prader-Willi syndrome, Angelman syndrome, and epilepsy.

In 1998, a study that appeared in the academic magazine The Lancet revealed a connection between childhood vaccination and autism as a possible cause of the disorder. The scientific community and parents rapidly disagreed with this notion, turning it into a contentious topic. Scientific data gathered from comprehensive investigations looking into the hypothesized linkage, however, did not establish a causal link. The 1998 manuscript was withdrawn by the journal in 2010 after further examinations found that it had breached research ethics and included fraudulent assertions.

Symptoms and signs

Autism may present with a range of mild, moderate, and severe signs and symptoms. There are three main groups of symptoms and signs:
 (1) abnormalities in social contact;
(2) abnormalities in communication; and
(3) abnormalities in behaviors, interests, and activities—usually constrained and repetitive—are all examples of aberrant behavior. A limited range of facial emotions, ineffective eye contact, and trouble building connections with peers are all examples of social communication issues. If this is badly impacted, it may lead to a decline in the quality of their interactions and, in some cases, social avoidance. Delay in or absence of

spoken language, poor conversational skills, a lack of developmental play that is appropriate, and decreased gestures are all examples of communication issues.

Problems with repetitive behavior include stereotyped motor behaviors like hand flapping, constrained interests, rigid adherence to routines, and an obsession with the individual components of items. For example, a kid with autism may play with the wheels of a toy car instead of operating the automobile in the right way as a vehicle. Some kids develop intense attachments to certain things, like buttons, and become fascinated with them. Additionally, disruptions to schedules and habits or too comfortable environments may result in irritation and tantrums.

The majority of kids with autism also have atypical eating habits, such as excessive sensitivity to food textures and extremely specific dietary preferences. Children who are affected, for instance, could choose meals that have a certain color or might only choose grains. This behavior may be visible as early as one year of age.

Neuropathology
Studies of autistic children and postmortem examinations of autistic people in the 1970s and 1980s revealed links between autism and insignificant physical abnormalities such as increased body size, expanded

head circumference, and increased brain weight. A significant portion of brain development connected to autism and other ASDs seems to happen before the age of two, according to a later study comparing the rates of brain growth between people with ASD and healthy people. In older autistic children, the early phase of overgrowth is followed by a phase of delayed or average development, leading to a normal or slightly bigger brain volume. In certain situations, overgrowth is seen as early as one to two months after delivery.

However, early development abnormalities, such as an increased head circumference, are not always associated with autism, and evidence suggests that if they do occur, these abnormalities are more likely to affect males than girls. The odd overgrowth pattern may be brought on by an expansion of the white matter of the brain, which contains the nerve fibers that link one part of the brain to another. The temporal lobe is one area of the brain where excessive white matter expansion has been seen. The Wernicke area, a cluster of motor neurons involved in speech comprehension, is located in the temporal lobe, a region with expertise in the processing of auditory inputs.

The cerebellum, a motor and cognitive brain region, the anterior cingulate cortex, a part of the cerebral cortex that is important for social and emotional behavior, and the hippocampus, an area important for learning and memory, have all been examined in other studies of the neuropathology of brain structures in autistic people. These brain areas often show decreased cell size and increased cell density in autistic youngsters. Purkinje cells, which receive and integrate information from sensory and motor neurons, are also frequently reduced in the cerebellum.

Numerous studies have examined the role of neurotransmitter systems in autism, and many have shown that the serotonin (5-HT) and inhibitory gamma-aminobutyric acid (GABA) systems are involved. Early observations of elevated serotonin levels in the peripheral blood (hyperserotonemia) in many autistic people prompted researchers to look into whether comparable brain abnormalities exist. It is yet unknown how the serotonin neurotransmitter system may contribute to the signs and symptoms of autism. Investigation of an allegedly uncommon human CELF6 gene mutation has provided some new information. This gene's loss of activity in mice has been associated with dramatic drops in serotonin levels and behaviors resembling autism, such as difficulties communicating and learning.

There is ample evidence that several areas of the autistic human brain have altered GABA and GABA receptor levels. Glutamic acid decarboxylases 67 and 65, two important GABA-synthesizing enzymes, are changed in particular cerebellar neurons in autistic brains. A third to one-third of adolescents with autism exhibit some kind of atypical seizure behavior, according to studies, and this is thought to be connected to GABA system problems.

Some persons with autism have fewer neural connections stretching from the frontal lobe to other brain areas than healthy people, according to earlier research on brain anatomy. Functional magnetic resonance imaging was used to identify deficits in neuronal transmission and the strength of connections between the frontal lobe and other parts of the brain (fMRI). Variations in the gene known as contactin-associated protein-like 2 (CNTNAP2), which is usually expressed in the frontal lobe throughout development and promotes neural connection, have been related to structural and functional abnormalities in the frontal lobe of autistic people. Some of the behavioral indications and symptoms seen in early childhood with autism may be explained by CNTNAP2 mutations that result in a loss of neural connection since the frontal lobe is linked to higher cognitive abilities, such as reasoning and emotion processing.

Chapter 2

What causes autism in kids.

There is no way to pinpoint the precise origin of your child's autism since autism spectrum disorder (ASD) has no established etiology. In actuality, it is widely believed that ASD is caused by a combination of factors. Instead, other variables might raise a child's risk.

Two elements that are thought to influence a child's risk of having ASD are genetics and environment. A child's probability of developing a pervasive developmental problem rising by 2% to 20% if an older sibling has an autistic impairment suggests that genetics may play a significant impact.

The developmental circumstances of the kid in the womb are frequent potential environmental factors. For instance, "advanced parental age at the time of conception" and "prenatal exposure to air pollution or particular pesticides" are two potential risk factors listed by the U.S. National Institute of Environmental Health Sciences. Research, however, indicates that whether or not a kid may acquire autism is mostly determined by genetics. Instead, experts emphasize genetics and keep looking into precisely which genes might alter to cause autism.

Parents and other caregivers must put the child's future ahead of their own, regardless of the probable reason. A kid that is born without autism is unlikely to "acquire" it as they mature since the available research indicates that autism tends to develop at a young age.

Finding evidence-based autism therapy that can assist the family in adjusting and the kid in thriving is the best answer to an autism diagnosis.
Genetic or medical testing cannot be used to diagnose ASD.
The fact that all of the causative theories are speculative should be one of the first things people know about the potential "cause" of ASD.

For instance, there is presently no genetic test for ASD, even though medical experts are aware that having a sibling, parent, or another close relative with autism might up a child's relative risk. A startling 102 genes that may be linked to ASD were also discovered by one of the greatest in-depth investigations of genetics in people with autism.

Similar to how sensory disorders, a frequent co-occurring illness in people with autism, have different brain structures, research has not yet shown a consistent pattern of abnormalities in the brain scans of juvenile ASD patients.These studies demonstrate that ASD may have reasons that are as complicated and varied as the individuals who have it. Risk factors should be understood by parents, but they should place a greater emphasis on what needs to be done to satisfy the child's needs now that an ASD diagnosis has been made.

What Elements of the Environment Might Increase the Risk of Autism?
Researchers have hypothesized several environmental elements that might increase a child's chance of developing autism. It's important to remember that although these characteristics have been shown to have little impact on the likelihood of getting autism, they are still there.

These consist of:
birthing the kid at a young age
extreme underweight at birth.

Exposure to contaminants during pregnancy.
pregnancy-related infections
birth prematurely.
These environmental influences all tend to have an impact on the fetus's brain development while it is still in the womb.

The National Institute of Neurological Disorders and Stroke states that "studies imply that ASD might be caused by disturbances in normal brain growth very early in life." These anomalies "may be the consequence of errors in genes that affect brain cell communication and influence brain development."Once again, the impact of environmental influences is purely hypothetical. There haven't been any studies that back up assertions about one or more components. This applies to the purported association between vaccination and autism, which has been debunked by more than 25 research.

Why Are There Now More Children With ASD Diagnoses?

The fact that the prevalence of autism diagnoses in youngsters has, by all accounts, increased is one of the reasons some parents and interest groups claim they wish to look for a cause of the disorder.
According to a study of the literature from the early 2000s, juvenile autism prevalence surged by 556% between 1991 and 1997, surpassing spina bifida, cancer, and Down syndrome in prevalence.

But according to the same research, rather than new environmental impacts, "this surge is largely linked to heightened awareness and shifting diagnostic criteria."

One can follow the development of the diagnosis of autism alongside advancements as recent as the 2013 release of the Diagnostic and Statistical Manual of Mental Disorders (DSM-5) fifth edition.
Before the release of the 5th edition, a kid with autism may alternatively be labeled with Asperger's syndrome, childhood disintegrative disorder, or an unidentified kind of pervasive developmental disability (PDD-NOS).
Now, the whole range of these potential manifestations is referred to as autism (ASD). The word "spectrum"

is particularly important to psychologists since two children with ASD will likely have quite diverse needs and experiences.

Anyone who is still focused on the increase in autism diagnoses should be aware that this simply implies that many autistic individuals were either undetected or given a different diagnosis.As a result, it is possible that millions of autistic persons in the previous century or so did not get the proper care and therapy. Focus on the fact that care choices for people with autism have significantly improved in tandem with the growth in diagnostic frequency rather than worrying about the cause of the disorder.

Providing Your Child with the Best Care to Aid in Their Development

After your kid has been diagnosed with autism, you may take efforts to determine their needs and seek to address them via proactive therapy. Autism-related children may need care and environmental modifications. Additionally, learning coping mechanisms for a range of circumstances might assist parents and children avoid undesirable consequences.

Anyone with autism may be provided with the circumstances they need to develop into their best selves with the proper approach.

Chapter 3

Problematic actions in autistic kids

Children with autism spectrum disorder exhibit abnormal behavior, ranging from eating problems to self-harm, since the illness directly interferes with brain development. When it comes to dealing with challenging behaviors, behavioral analysis and understanding parents are crucial components of a child who has autism. Even though there may be several causes for these alternative behaviors, they may be stopped with the right functional analysis and instruction.

Problems with behavior abnormalities in autistic children might also entail deprivation. When their regular pattern is disturbed, they could lose their anger and act violently. These disruptive behaviors might have a variety of causes. These kid actions may indicate that the child is avoiding or dislikes a certain job in addition to having biological and psychological causes. Parents in this scenario should keep an eye on the right actions. It is important to acquaint the kid with the issue first if it is a functional behavioral topic; otherwise, the child's conduct shouldn't be forced.

How to Respond to Autism's Changing Behaviors

Autism issues should be changed gradually and cautiously.

During autism treatment, establishing goal behaviors and making incremental adjustments to them is a safe and effective approach to use. Instantaneous problem-solving attempts may erode a child's respect for and tolerance of parents. Since the youngster is not active, eating habits that were developed over time may also result in fat and excess weight. A healthy diet is crucial for those with various types of behavioral issues.

Understand the rationale for the use of behavior

Children with autism often exhibit behaviors that are seen as abnormal for a variety of reasons. To catch their parent's attention, kids could, for instance, engage in harmful conduct like tossing things across the room or making loud sounds. This is only the effect of trying to get attention. However, the youngster should be led gradually to limit and diminish these undesirable behaviors. This raises the probability of constructive activity.

Children with autism may weep or complain when they want to avoid or stop doing an activity they do not enjoy, just like any other kid. If these actions become habitual, the person in question has to be patiently spoken to and comforted.

The youngster may dislike hundreds of circumstances and actions at school or home. To prevent them, parents should identify and make a list of the circumstances and actions that make their children shout and become restless. It is important to thoroughly evaluate the environmental influences that have an impact on the kid. The youngster might then use his or her emotions as a means of communication.

Problematic Behavior and Its Treatment in Autistic Children

Regarding the Treatment of Conduct Disorder Parents and professionals should carefully identify the most crucial factors after compiling a list of the child's problematic behaviors and then take appropriate action. If the youngster has acquired a habit of biting himself or others around him, the most detrimental behaviors, like that, should be addressed first. Parents and specialists should maintain their composure during therapy and beyond, and the recommended course of action should be followed regularly. Every environment must adhere to this consistency for the child's education to be successful and for the behavior to be retained. A good education will help the autistic youngster adjust to regular life and make any future challenges much easier to deal with. The youngster may even improve the quality of his life further by pursuing a higher degree, allowing him to live a more comfortable life for both himself and his parents.

Everybody has fundamental wants, including those for food, drink, sleep, and release from unpleasant circumstances. We yearn for entertainment and have preferences for various people, locations, and things. Most usually developing individuals begin to learn how to communicate their wants to others as early as infancy. A person could not have the essential communication skills to express his demands in a socially acceptable manner if a communication issue like autism spectrum disorder (ASD) is present.

Aggression, property damage, self-injury, fleeing, and yelling or sobbing are a few of the troublesome behaviors connected to ASD. Others could involve repeated motions like back-and-forth rocking or hand flapping. Higher functioning individuals with ASD may exhibit fewer overtly problematic behaviors

but yet engage in actions that negatively affect effective social engagement.
Unwanted habits are acquired via learned experience. When a problematic behavior takes place and is reinforced (like yelling for snacks in the grocery store), the likelihood of it happening again rises because it is beneficial to the person in some manner.

It might be beneficial to think about the motivation behind a troublesome behavior and the function it serves. Say a kid is craving sweets from the supermarket. The parent refuses, the kid screams, and the parent then buys the sweets. The little toddler has just discovered that yelling at people to gain sweets. There may be other methods to get sweets, but if tantruming is the simplest and most successful one, it will probably occur once again. Add ASD to the mix, and it's possible that the youngster may not be able to vocally request a treat or will not comprehend when the parent says "no, it's nearly time for dinner." Now it's much simpler to see how a tantrum might become the easiest option.

Think about what occurs just before and before the activity, and perhaps more crucial, what occurs immediately after. The individual either receives something or attracts someone's attention. Is a bad action abstained from? Or is it conceivable that the behavior—like rocking back and forth—is just satisfying physically? We are more likely to be able to create an effective reaction to stop a behavior if we know why it is happening.

Parents, teachers, and other caregivers can react to troublesome behavior inadvertently in a manner that ultimately does more damage than good. Think about a young person who is having difficulty in class. He regularly gets reprimanded, the task is challenging, and the other students don't like him because of his frequent disruptions. He disturbs class and is taken to the principal's office. Maybe he chooses to go the extra mile and have a leisurely walk down the corridor before having a little chat with someone outside the office and returning just in time for the ring. This youngster has just discovered a means to get out of class, so the teacher's well-intended punishment is likely to have the unexpected result of making him even more unruly. For this kid, a better strategy may be to break down his homework and give him additional help so that it is not so overwhelming, to give him plenty of social praise for engaging correctly, and to give him the chance to earn breaks for being on track.

While difficult to deal with, troublesome conduct is surmountable. An informal strategy that may be utilized with any problematic behavior, whether it is connected to ASD or not, is the attempt to ascertain why behavior is taking place, as explained in this article.

It may be beneficial to hire a Board Certified Behavior Analyst, or BCBA, in more severe circumstances. These people have received training in applied behavior analysis (ABA), a discipline that studies how to alter socially significant behavior by adjusting environmental factors and evaluating the results. They may carry out more formal evaluations to ascertain the purpose of behavior and assist parents, carers, and educators in creating effective solutions.

Chapter 4

Recognize and help your child.

If you just found out that your kid has autism spectrum disorder or may have it, you're undoubtedly wondering and fretting about what happens next. A diagnosis of ASD may be especially terrifying since no parent is ever ready to learn that their kid is anything other than happy and healthy. You could be perplexed by contradictory treatment recommendations or unaware of how to best assist your kid. You could also be afraid that nothing you do will change since you've been informed that ASD is an incurable, lifelong disorder.

Even while it's true that ASD isn't something a person just "grows out of," there are several therapies that may assist kids in learning new abilities and overcoming a broad range of developmental obstacles. To fulfill your child's specific needs and enable them to learn, develop, and flourish in life, support is available, including free government services, in-home behavioral treatment, and school-based programs.

It's crucial to look after yourself while caring for a child with autism. Being emotionally resilient enables you to provide the greatest care possible for your kid. These parenting hints may ease the burden of raising a kid who has autism.

Stop waiting for a diagnosis.

As the parent of a kid with ASD or associated developmental delays, the best thing you can do is to start therapy immediately early. As soon as you suspect a problem, get assistance. Don't hold off to see whether your youngster will eventually catch up or outgrow the issue. Waiting for a formal diagnosis is unnecessary. The better the possibility of treatment success for children with autism spectrum conditions, the sooner they get assistance. The best strategy to accelerate a child's growth and lessen autism symptoms over time is via early intervention.

Having an autistic kid

Study up on autism. The more knowledgeable you are about autism spectrum conditions, the more able you will be to make choices for your kid. Ask questions, become knowledgeable about the available treatments, and take part in choosing your treatment.

Gain expertise in your child. Find out what causes your child's difficult or disruptive behaviors and what makes them go away. What frightens or stresses your child? Calming? Uncomfortable? Enjoyable? Understanding how your kid is affected can help you solve issues more effectively and avoid or alter challenging circumstances.

Embrace your child's differences. Practice acceptance rather than concentrating on how your autistic child differs from other kids and what he or she is "missing." Enjoy your child's unique traits, acknowledge tiny victories, and refrain from comparing your child to others. More than anything else, your kid will benefit from feeling welcomed and loved unconditionally.

Never give up. The trajectory of the autism spectrum condition cannot be predicted. Don't assume anything about how your child's life will turn out. People with autism have a lifetime to mature and hone their skills, just like everyone else.

Tip #1 for raising an autistic child: Establish structure and safety
Your kid will benefit greatly from your involvement in therapy and your efforts to learn as much as you can about autism. The following advice can also help you and your kid with ASD live more comfortably at home:

Be dependable. Children with ASD struggle to transfer their knowledge from one environment, like the classroom or therapist's office, to another, like their home. For instance, your kid could communicate with you at home using sign language, but not at school. The most effective strategy to support learning is to provide stability in your child's surroundings. Learn what the therapists are doing with your kid and use the same methods at home. To help your kid apply what he or she has learned from one setting to another, consider having treatment take place in more than one location. It's crucial to maintain consistency in how you speak to your kid and handle difficult behaviors.

Follow a timetable. Children with autism often do better when they follow a routine or timetable that is very regimented. This relates once again to the constancy they both need and want. Establish a routine for your child's meals, therapy sessions, school hours, and sleep. Try to limit the number of times this process is interrupted. If a schedule change is inevitable, have your youngster ready for it in advance.

Reward excellent conduct. With children with ASD, positive reinforcement may go a long way, so try to "catch them doing something nice." Be extremely explicit about the conduct you're praising them for when you congratulate them when they behave correctly or when they master a new ability. Consider other methods of rewarding them for excellent conduct, such as letting them play with a favorite item or giving them a sticker.

Make your house a safe place. Create a personal area in your home where your child can unwind, feel safe, and feel secure. This calls for structuring and establishing limits in a manner that your youngster can comprehend. Visual clues may be useful (colored tape marking areas that are off limits, labeling items in the house with pictures). Additionally, you may want to safety-proof your home, especially if your kid is prone to tantrums or other self-harming behaviors.

Tip 2: Look for nonverbal cues to communicate.
It may be difficult to connect with a kid who has autism, but you don't need to speak to them or even touch them to do so. Your body language, tone of voice, how you look at your kid, and sometimes even how you touch them are all ways that you can connect with them. Even if your kid never talks, they are talking with you anyway. You merely need to learn the language.

Observe any nonverbal indications. You may learn to recognize the nonverbal clues that autistic children use to communicate if you are attentive and aware. When a person is weary, hungry, or in need of anything, you may tell by the noises they make, their facial expressions, and the actions they make.

Determine the cause of the temper tantrum. When you are misunderstood or disregarded, it's only normal to feel sad, and this is also true for children with ASD. Children with ASD often act out when you fail to notice their nonverbal signs, according to research. Their method of expressing their annoyance and demanding your attention is through tantruming.

Schedule an enjoyable time. Despite having ASD, a kid is still a child. There must be more to life than treatment for parents and children with autism. Decide when your kid will be most awake and attentive for fun. Consider the things that make your kid laugh, smile, and come out of her/his shell as you try to come up with methods to have fun together. If these activities don't appear therapeutic or instructional, your youngster is most likely to enjoy them. Both you and your kid will gain a lot by taking pleasure in one another's presence and spending time together unhurriedly. All children need to play to learn, and it shouldn't seem like work.

Keep an eye out for your child's sensory needs. Many kids with ASD have extreme sensitivity to touch, sound, light, smell, and taste. Some autistic children exhibit "under-sensitivity" to sensory stimuli. Analyze your child's "bad" or disruptive actions to see what sights, sounds, scents, movements, and tactile sensations they are drawn to, as well as what makes them feel good. What causes stress in your child? Calming? Uncomfortable? Enjoyable? You'll be more adept at solving issues, avoiding sticky situations, and fostering positive experiences if you know what impacts your kid.

Make a specialized autism treatment strategy (tip 3).

It might be difficult to decide which therapy is best for your kid when there are so many options available. You can get various or even contradicting advice from your parents, professors, and physicians, further complicating the situation.

Remember that no one therapy is effective for everyone when creating a treatment plan for your kid. Every autistic individual is distinct, with their unique talents and shortcomings.

The course of therapy for your kid should be personalized for their particular need. It is up to you to see that their needs are satisfied since you are the one who knows your kid the best. You may achieve it by asking the following questions yourself:

What are the advantages and disadvantages of my child?

Which actions are the most problematic? What crucial abilities does my kid lack?

Which kind of learning is better for my child: watching, listening, or doing?

What activities does my kid want to perform, and how can we utilize them in therapy and support learning?

Finally, remember that your participation is essential to the success of any treatment strategy, regardless of the one selected. By collaborating with the treatment team and completing the therapy at home, you can ensure that your kid gets the most out of their treatment. (This is why it's crucial to prioritize your health!)

Build on your child's interests in a successful therapeutic strategy.
Provide a foreseeable timetable.
Teach things in small, manageable increments.
Engage your child's interest directly in activities that are quite organized.
Give behavior reinforcement regularly.
Participate in the parent's.
selecting autism therapies
Behavioral therapy, speech-language therapy, physical therapy, occupational therapy, and nutritional therapy are just a few of the various treatments and methods used to treat ASD.

It's doubtful that you'll be able to treat all of your kid's issues at once, even while you're not required to restrict your child to just one therapy at a time. Instead, begin by concentrating on your child's urgent needs and most severe symptoms.

Tip 4: Look for aid and assistance
Taking care of a kid with autism may take a lot of time and effort. There may be times when you feel anxious, disheartened, or overburdened. Raising a kid with special needs is significantly harder than parenting a typical youngster. You must look after yourself if you want to be the best parent you can be.

Don't attempt to do everything by yourself. You're not required to! Families of children with ASD have a variety of resources at their disposal for guidance, assistance, advocacy, and support:

ASD support groups - Attending an ASD support group is a terrific opportunity to connect with other families going through similar struggles. Parents may rely on one another for emotional support, information sharing, and guidance. The loneliness many parents face after learning their kid has a diagnosis may sometimes be much diminished by just being with others who are in the same situation and listening to their stories.

services for early intervention (birth through age two)

The Early Intervention program offers support to young children up to the age of two. Your kid must first go through a free assessment to be eligible. You will collaborate with early intervention therapy professionals to create an individualized family service plan if the evaluation identifies a developmental issue (IFSP). Your child's requirements and the exact services he or she will receive are detailed in an IFSP.

An IFSP for autism would include various play, physical, speech, and behavior therapy. It would concentrate on getting autistic children ready for the eventual transition to school. Early intervention services are often provided at home or in a daycare facility. Ask your physician for a recommendation, or utilize the resources provided in the Resources section after the article, to find nearby early intervention options for your child.

services for special education (age three and older)

Assistance is provided to children over three via school-based initiatives. Special education programs are adapted to your child's unique requirements, much as early intervention. Children with autism are often put in small groups with other children who have developmental delays so that they may get more individualized care and specialized training. But they may also spend at least part of the school day in a conventional classroom, depending on their skills. The idea is to put children in the "least restrictive setting" they can be in while still learning.

If you think your child's needs are not being fulfilled, you may request an IEP meeting at any time.

If you can't reach a compromise with the school, you may get free or inexpensive legal assistance.

Taking care of a kid with autism while having autism

According to research, autism has a hereditary component. But many parents don't learn they have autism until after they do their research and get an official diagnosis for their kid. If you have autism, parenting children who are also neurodivergent may present special difficulties for you. The following advice might be helpful:

Don't conceal who you are. Allow your youngster to see who you are. Don't feel forced to hide any peculiar habits or bodily motions you may have from your kid if you have them. By being yourself, you give your autistic kid permission to be authentic around you and provide the two of you a chance to connect through shared interests. You may also discuss with your kid how neurotypical others could respond to your activities and how to manage unfavorable responses. Try to provide advice that you may have benefited from when you were younger.

Always take good care of yourself. If you suffer from sensory requirements or need a highly regimented lifestyle, caring for a kid might be difficult. A crying child, for instance, might be a constant source of stress and discomfort if you're sensitive to sounds. You may find it challenging to maintain a routine due to a child's unplanned tantrums, which will only make you more frustrated. You must develop coping mechanisms that may help you feel less stressed in these kinds of circumstances if you want to safeguard your feeling of well-being.

Look for assistance from others if certain jobs seem too difficult to do. For instance, a parenting mentor or other parents of children with autism may be able to assist you to come up with solutions if talking with physicians and teachers is difficult.

accentuate your advantages. Everyone has unique strengths, and you are no different. Think about how your abilities may assist you in creating a nurturing environment for your kid. Do you excel in visual thinking or design? For your youngster, create instructive posters. Can you maintain sustained concentration? Utilize that concentration to learn more about parenting techniques and coping mechanisms. Are you adept at problem-solving? To solve problems around the home, utilize your imagination and innovative thinking.

Both you and your kid deserve your patience. Recognize that you both have a lot of room to develop and learn. There might be some setbacks. You may lose your anger and feel embarrassed by your behavior. Or maybe your kid struggles to blend in with their classmates when they first start school. Decide to learn from mistakes and discover answers, even if it takes a few tries. Remember to recognize progress when one of you does do it. Praise your youngster and acknowledge your accomplishments as well.

Chapter 5

Controlling an autistic child's emotions

Autism And The Self-Regulation Of Emotions:

A collection of abilities and/or methods known as self-regulation may aid us in maintaining control over our feelings and actions. Self-regulation, in the words of McClelland & Tominey (2014), "involves conscious control of ideas, emotions, and actions." Children's bodies exhibit indicators of dysregulation when they are "bouncing off the walls" or acting out in tantrums. It could be brought on by being too exhausted, excited, frustrated, upset, or several other things. Young children have a constrained capacity for self-control. They initially practice co-regulating with the adults in their surroundings before starting to learn how to control their emotions on their own. Modeling and prompting abilities that might assist a kid in regaining control when they are becoming dysregulated are a part of co-regulation.

Simple exercises like simulating deep breaths might be used for this (not telling the child to take deep breaths). These techniques must be taught to children while their bodies and minds are calm and under control. To make it "easier" to access that skill when dysregulating, for instance, have activities where you practice deep breathing when you are calm.

How to Help Young Children with Autism Learn to Control Their Emotions

#1 The grownups around the youngsters must maintain their composure. We won't be able to educate the kid to self-regulate if we, as adults, are unable to do so and model such behavior. Adults must maintain their composure throughout the co-regulation period. Children are said to be able to sense someone's "vibe" frequently. When it comes to the co-regulation and self-regulation of emotions, this is true! When we are anxious, agitated, or disappointed, a youngster may sense it. Therefore, the best course of action is to first check in with ourselves to ensure that we are modeling deep breathing and other self-regulation techniques. An agitated youngster cannot be calmed down by an agitated adult.

#2 You should be modeling, encouraging, and reinforcing the self-regulation techniques as an adult. The first tip mentioned this. In actuality, it can include demonstrating slow, deep breathing next to the youngster without soliciting or requesting their participation. If you keep doing it, ultimately their breathing will match yours. Co-regulation may be seen in this situation. Hugs and cuddles are other examples of co-regulation when youngsters are unhappy, angry, or overstimulated. As they go toward developing their self-regulation of emotions, preschoolers will need varying degrees of co-regulation.

#3 Teaching children about emotions directly can be very beneficial. For kids with autism, being able to recognize emotions may be a challenging task. Use flashcards with line drawings or clipart images of emotions to begin teaching the fundamental emotions. Teach your kid or student how to recognize, express, and classify fundamental emotions. The greatest place to start sometimes is happy, sad, and furious. You may then proceed to mimic those feelings by making faces in the mirror together. Other enjoyable activities include making faces out of play dough and drawing faces with various emotions on paper or a small whiteboard. Once your student or child is familiar with the fundamentals of emotion, be sure to start identifying them in everyday situations. For instance, you may use the phrase "they feel sad" if a youngster is sobbing at the grocery store. Learning to self-regulate emotions may be aided by an understanding of emotions.

#4 When language is dysregulated, make it simpler. It is more difficult for a youngster to use their "thinking" abilities when their body and mind are stressed and dysregulated. When speaking to children who are suffering dysregulation, it is crucial to utilize simple language. Specify fewer instructions and talk in a lower, more relaxed tone. This aids in the co-regulation topic that was covered in earlier advice.

Use visual aids, number five. One of the finest methods for assisting kids in transitioning from co-regulation to self-regulation of emotions is the use of visual aids. Using visual aid to educate and promote deep breathing is one instance of this. You practice this deep breathing with them when they are calm and in a state of regulation so that they may use it more naturally when they are experiencing dysregulation. "Smell the flower...blow out the candle," for instance (see below). The teaching of a soothing sequence is no different. While in a controlled, calm state, practice a calming sequence several times per day. The youngster will then find it simpler to access that ability when they are starting to exhibit dysregulation.

Tool Repair

The emotional repair mechanisms of autistic children and adults may be limited, and they are less likely to employ successful techniques used by typical children and adults, such as perspective-taking, reappraising the circumstance, considering potential responses, acceptance, or being able to disclose feelings to another person, thereby benefiting from empathy, validation, and affection from a family member or friend. Children and adults with autism may acquire new emotion repair techniques, which can be thought of as obtaining additional emotion repair tools.

Children learn very early that a toolbox contains a variety of tools that can be used to fix a machine or a domestic issue. Finding various "tools" to address the issues brought on by unpleasant emotions, particularly worry, is the technique. Children and adults with autism might be thought of as having an "energy management" issue, which involves having too much emotional energy and having trouble managing and releasing it healthily. Autistic people often seek to solve or release the sensation by an active, perhaps damaging activity or thinking and emotion-blocking action because they tend to be less able to gradually release emotional energy through rest and introspection.

The range of tools can be broken down into those that swiftly and productively release, or gradually reduce, emotional energy, and those that improve thinking or reduce sensory responsiveness, as well as removing those tools that can exacerbate the emotions or consequences, such as self-harm, from the toolbox.

Actual Tools
Tools or behaviors that physically release emotional energy via a positive and appropriate activity are represented by a hammer. This may involve jumping on a trampoline, riding a swing, or utilizing playground

equipment for young autistic children. Although a school may provide these amenities, a student with autism may choose not to utilize them because of the number of students utilizing the same equipment and the student's desire for isolation and avoidance of social contacts during break periods. They could be given a special pass to use this equipment while the other kids are in class. It is simpler to promote such physical activity as an emotional recovery technique at home.

Unfortunately, autistic children and adults sometimes feel awkward and uncoordinated, and they really could be. They have also frequently endured bullying in the past for being bad in team sports and ball games from peers. Although studies have shown that physical activity reduces autistic children's repetitive behavior, aggressiveness, inattentiveness, and escape behaviors (Lang et al., 2010), there may be a poor desire for and self-confidence in physical activities. A personal trainer may be able to determine the body type and personality of the kid or adult and create a tailored program of practical and doable physical exercises that can be accomplished in private and don't entail social situations where there is a danger of scorn. We understand that regular exercise is fantastic for both physical and mental health, as well as for enhancing mental acuity and problem-solving skills. We communicate the idea that "exercise will make you smarter" to autistic kids and adults because they often appreciate and want to show off their intellectual prowess.

Destruction is a physical technique that some autistic children and adults have discovered may be a highly efficient "fast cure" to alleviate uncomfortable sensations of repressed or intensifying anxiety, despair, and rage. Some household tasks can be completed at home that satisfies the urge to be destructive without resulting in damage that might need to be repaired out of pocket. For instance, used clothing may be broken up to form rags, or empty cans, water bottles, or boxes can be crushed for recycling. This "creative devastation" may be the go-to mending method at home, particularly after coming from work or school.

Tools for Relaxation

Normal kids and adults typically have an innate understanding of how to unwind because it is a state of mind that they have frequently encountered. With someone who has autism, this may not be the case. Our significant therapeutic experience has shown that when someone tells you to "just relax," there are often difficulties entering that condition as well as misunderstandings about what to do.

The use of relaxation techniques aids in lowering heart rate as well as the progressive release and reduction of emotional energy. This group of instruments for emotional restoration might be represented by an image of a paintbrush or a spirit level. Drawing, reading, and—perhaps most importantly—listening to relaxing music may all be used as relaxation techniques or hobbies to help you progressively let go of anxious thoughts and anxieties. When routine tasks or activities are finished, they might bring about feelings of achievement, contentment, and relaxation.

Autism is characterized by the fact that solitude—as opposed to loneliness—is a highly effective way to unwind. Being alone and away from certain sensory stimuli, such as retiring to a peaceful, isolated sanctuary, may often help individuals relax and heal their emotions while lowering worry and tension. Both in school or job and at home, the autistic person will need islands of peace. The autistic student's parent or teacher may be able to arrange for the autistic student to use a quiet area of the school during recess or break times, such as the library. Such solitude can be emotionally reviving and a way to truly unwind. Being outside, strolling, or camping in a natural setting, with limited social interactions and just natural sensory experiences, and interacting with the animals may be additional sources of relaxation.

A helpful technique for mending broken emotions is cue-controlled relaxation. The plan is for the individual to carry an item, maybe concealed in their pocket, that, by association, denotes and fosters emotions of serenity and peace. A fishing float in a pocket may be retrieved and examined to reenact the sentiments, sights, and sensations of calm and satisfaction while fishing, for instance, for an autistic youngster who may feel at ease when on vacation and fishing.

Tools for Meditation

Growing understanding and appreciation of the benefits of practices like yoga and meditation in promoting overall well-being and acting as an antidote to worry are seen in Western cultures. There are now yoga exercises designed specifically for autistic children to practice at home and school (Betts & Betts, 2006; Bolls & Sewell, 2013; Mitchell 2014; Hardy, 2015), and some teachers are implementing group and individual meditation exercises to promote calmness and improved focus for the entire class. Utilizing images, meditation, and yoga, mindfulness is also used to control the attention on the present moment, let an emotion pass, and promote an attitude of openness and acceptance (De Bruin et al., 2015).

9 798353 053712